INTRODUCT

For years I have sewn straight. Accurate measurements, precise cutting lines, precision seam allowances, symmetric topstitching and decorative stitching were all in the basic plan in my sewing. Everything had to be just so—perfect.

As I began to work on my first book, **Texture With Textiles**, I started to explore a variety of embellishments to combine different areas of sewing—metallic with rayon, heirloom with quick piecing, flat, shiny fabrics with textured or napped fabrics. I discovered the thrill of being creative. With my collection of fabrics, threads, trims, laces, buttons, beads, and ribbons, I observed that I no longer demanded perfection in my work; that errors could turn into designer touches; that it is more relaxing to enjoy my sewing now that I can break a few rules.

Though many lines in **Texture With Textiles** were straight, I began to develop uneven patterns. I discovered it is more fun to sew a crooked line than it is to sew straight, and that feet are available for every machine to make applications easier and more accurate. I discovered that it was okay to hide a mistake with another embellishment rather than to rip it out. I finally realized that nothing has to be perfect.

As I begin my second venture in texture, I remind myself and you that no one is flawless. It is more fun to sew from that point of view. I am a reformed perfectionist and my sewing can be as much fun and as intense as I want it to be.

Enjoy a new adventure using your machine and all the toys that go along with it. Expand your horizons by experimenting with texture. Use equipment and accessories that will make it easier to explore new applications. Play with all the wonderful fabrics, threads, yarns, laces and trims that are available today.

TABLE OF CONTENTS

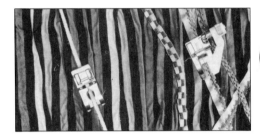

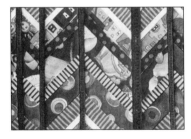

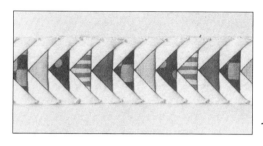

CREDITS

Author/Designer: Linda McGehee

Editing: Peri Caylor

Graphics & Layout: Digital Graphics, George Maimon

Photography: Scot Smith, Jack Williams

Sewing: Linda McGehee, Joyce West

Sewing Machine Feet: Babylock, Bernina, Creative Feet, Elna, Little Foot, Ltd., New Home, Pfaff, Singer, Viking

Batting & Interfacing: Fairfield Processing Corp.; HTC-Handler Textile Corp.; Hobbs Bonded Fibers; Staple Aids Sewing Corp.

Buttons: Albe Creations, Inc.; JHB International, Inc.

Dyes & Paints: Seitec: Sew Easy Industries; Jones Tones

Fabrics: Capitol Imports, Inc. of Tallahassee, FL; Chapel House Fabrics; Hoffman California Fabrics; Mary Ellen Hopkins; Jennifer Sampou, and Baltimore Beauties for P & B Fabrics; Quilting Plus by Wamsutta, a Division of Springs; Spiegel Fabrics

Laces, Ribbons & Trims: Capitol Imports, Inc. of Tallahassee, FL; Offray

Notions: Art's International, Inc.; Coats & Clark, Inc.; Glitz, Inc.; Quality Braid/Sequins USA

Patterns: Elizabeth Anne; Folkwear; Ghee's

Thread: Aardvark Adventures; Coats & Clark, Inc.; Gutermann of America, Inc.; Kreinik Mfg. Co. Inc.; Madeira Marketing Ltd.; Swiss Metrosene, Inc.; Sulky of America; YLI Corp.

Crinkling in **Texture With Textiles** was completed by wetting fabric, gathering it from selvage to selvage, and twisting it until the fabric starts to roll on top of itself. Rubber bands or string were used to hold the twists in place and the fabric was dried **(photo 1)**. Once the wet fabric dried, the piece was opened to show wonderful wrinkles that were interfaced to a fusible interfacing. The interfacing made the wrinkles into a permanent crinkled fabric. This type of gathering and twisting produced elongated tucks and pleats to be used as a base for further manipulation **(photo 2)**.

1

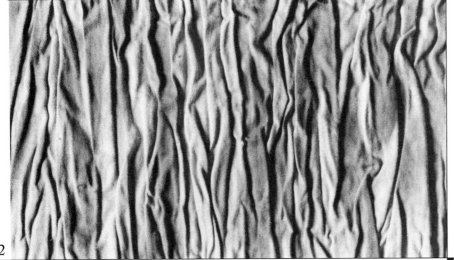

2

After working with these lengthwise tucks for awhile, we added extra rubber bands to the twisted wet cloth. Other times, the fabric was gathered from the center before twisting to produce a bull's-eye illusion **(photo**

3

3). This type of manipulation causes the fabric to shrink both in width and length **(photo 4)**. It is difficult to tell how much extra fabric is necessary for this technique. Just purchase more than necessary, in keeping with the theory that it is better to have too much than not enough. There are many small projects that use scraps; however, if there is minimal fabric to complete the project, more creativity may be needed than available.

Another experiment is to pour bleach over twisted denim (**photo 5**). Concentrate more bleach in some areas, while leaving other areas almost free of bleach. The idea is to completely whiten some areas of the fabric and combine color and white or pastel shades in other areas (**photo 6**). Bleaching time may vary depending on the fabric. Allow the fabric to rest between 15 minutes to one hour after bleaching it, then rinse it thoroughly several times with water to remove the bleach. Dry the crinkled, bleached fabric before applying to the interfacing (photo 7).

4

5

We also experimented with fabric dyes and paints on crinkled fabric. Muslin is a good basic for this (**page 10**). It is inexpensive and accepts the color nicely. The dyes were sprayed on the dry twisted fabric, and more dye was concentrated in some areas than in others to penetrate the fabric. After the twisted fabric has dried, we opened it slightly to apply the glitter paint. We used no particular rationale in positioning the paints or dyes; instead, we simply added another layer where too much base fabric was showing. Though we plan to do more dyeing and painting with the crinkled fabric, our current focus is on machine embellishments. Certainly, paints and dyes can enhance fabrics, and books

continues

are available for those who wish to learn more techniques for their application.

In experimenting with fabric, the possibilities are unlimited and the end products are always unique. I have never destroyed a piece of fabric, although some pieces look better than others. I have discovered that some fabrics look better crinkled than they did in the first place! Study your fabric collection. Crinkle fabrics that are otherwise unappealing. It is better to crinkle a fabric than to leave it in the closet. A new challenge begins when the fabric takes on a new dimension. Lighten up, experiment, and enjoy the adventure. Besides, you've already paid for the fabric.

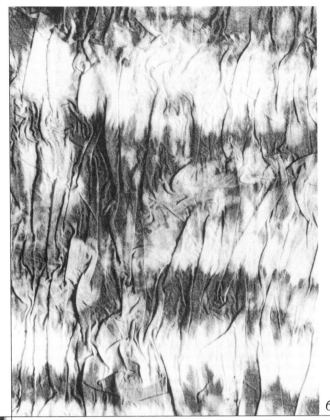

6

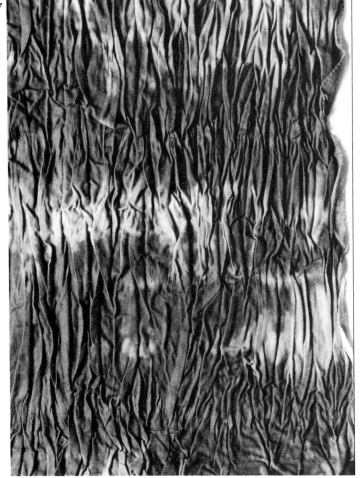

7

A new challenge begins when the fabric takes on a new dimension by crinkling

COUCHING & PINTUCKS

By definition, couching is a method of embroidery in which a design is created by hand or machine stitching over threads, cords, or yarns that have been arranged on the surface of a material. With the availability of more embellishments, such as sequins, beads, pearls and ribbons, and additional feet introduced by the machine companies, couching is taking a new dimension.

The market is overflowing with wonderful threads designed for the upper and lower loopers on sergers, yet heavy to use in the sewing machine needle. These metallic threads, braids, ombres and ribbons, pearl rayons and cottons, and other decorative yarns are perfect for couching. They glide through the foot maintaining their position making couching by machine a simple, quick process for creating an ornament or a trim (**photo 1**).

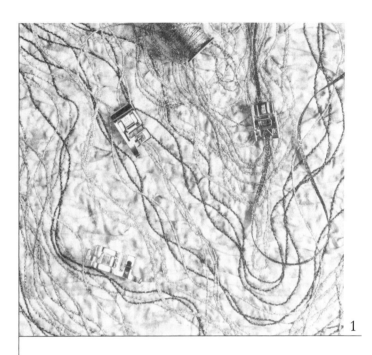

Cording feet with tiny grooves or holes through which three to seven heavier threads may pass allow many combinations of types and colors of thread. The different holes or grooves align the threads perfectly resulting in a ribbon illusion (**photo 2**). A subtle variegated design is achieved with slightly different shades of a color or a bolder appearance results with the sharper brighter colors. The possibilities are endless because a great variety of colors is available in the specialty threads.

A collection of these heavier threads may be twisted together like a candy cane and passed through the braiding foot for couching (**photo 3 left**). Much as with the process of making a cord, the threads may be one color or shades of a color. Another option is a combination of light and dark colors to create a barber pole effect.

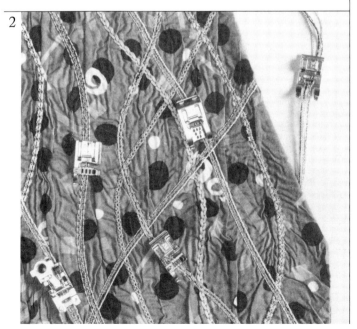

continues

Other choices in the creative process include determining the needle thread and type of stitch. Depending upon the decorative threads used in the foot choose a clear monofilament, rayon or metallic thread with appropriate size needle. Though a zigzag stitch may be used, the many exciting decorative stitches available with each new machine produce endless combinations. The honeycomb and serpentine stitches are two of my favorites.

Satin ribbon whether ⅛ or ¼ inch, is suitable for couching in a variety of ways. Use the braiding foot with the narrow ribbon, setting the decorative stitch width to allow the needle to go over the edge of the ribbon. Consider the daisy, ladder, or feather stitch for the narrow ribbon or any stitch that has open spaces, allowing the ribbon to show. Combinations of stitches are another alternative using the memory.

Continuing with (¼ inch) ribbon has more opportunities than ever. The edge-stitching **(photo 3 right)** foot permits accurate sewing along one edge. When the ribbon is couched in wavy

3

lines, the curves add extra dimension. Two rows of ribbon may be attached at one time, much like combining the laces with heirloom sewing. Both sides of the ribbon may be attached or one side left to float.

When a centered stitching is desired, use the open-toe embroidery foot **(photo 3 center)**. The ribbon fits perfectly between the toes of the foot, making accuracy a breeze. More open decorative stitches, staggered satin stitches, or the double needle with the feather stitch produce beautiful texture. Experiment with the stitch length and width for different effects. Be careful with the stitch width when using the double needle. The wider the distance between the needles, the narrower the width must be to prevent the needle from breaking. The double needle button on most new model machines allows the machine to stitch up to a certain width. Be sure to push the button.

4

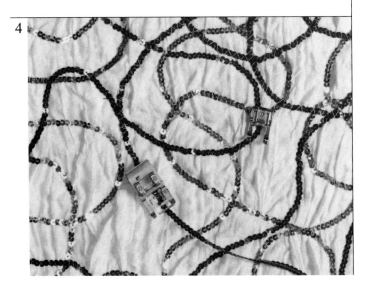

continues on page 13

Couching with ribbon, beading and
heavier threads on crinkled fabric,
denim and moiré

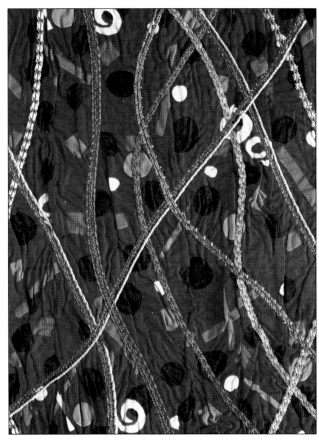

Crinkled muslin with fabric
dyes and paints create a
festive base for sequins and
other couching

Albe ceramic buttons add an individual touch • Bleached, crinkled denim with couched threads, ribbon, and woven rickrack • Fuzzies and tassels inserted in the cameo substitute for jewelry

Designed for special events during the year... Fourth of July and Mardi Gras

**Enlargements of P&B Fabric
and Chapel House Fabric
create wonderful appliqué
patterns**

continued from page 8

Add a festive appearance to any wearable by adding sequin yardage **(photo 4)**. Available in several widths and many colors, sequins are easily applied with the open toe foot, using the zigzag stitch and clear monofilament thread. Set the stitch width slightly wider than the sequin size, preventing the needle from piercing the sequin. The stitch length should be identical to the width. Because there is a nape to sequin yardage, the smooth direction should be placed so that it runs with the foot. If the sequins constantly catch on the foot, reverse the direction. They should glide through the foot without hesitation, making meandering stitching an elementary technique.

While many of the more open decorative stitches lend themselves to couching, so does double needle work. The main distraction with the double needle is

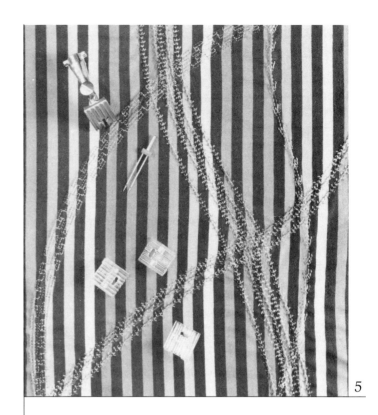

5

the stitch width capacity. Always test before stitching to be sure the needle clears the foot. Though much of the previous instruction for double needle pin tucks was in the round **(Texture With Textiles)**, it is possible to twist and turn the stitches roaming over the surface of the fabric **(photo 5)**. Consider sewing several close rows with the double needle and intersecting those rows with additional double stitching. The grooves in the pin tucking foot aid in producing perfect uniform tucks **(photo 6)**. These intersecting rows add a special effect. Some stitching may be corded. Others may be wider tucks with no cording.

Remember, there are no set rules. The possibilities are endless. Experiment with design and threads. Make a few mistakes. Discover another technique. Enjoy new freedom with the sewing machine.

6

13

*A*ppliqué has become one of the most recognized forms of embellishment. A design is applied to the surface of another fabric using hand or machine stitching, glue or fusing. You will find many appliqué patterns on the market, but you may also consider using the design in the fabric itself. Choose a basic design (**photo 1**). Eliminate some of the fine lines in the design. Enlarge the fabric on a copy machine. The shown design was enlarged 200%. The enlargement may be enlarged 200%. This is a simple way to produce an appliqué pattern. If you are artistic, feel free to draw designs. However, if you have limited time and prefer the appliqué to be an exact enlargement, use a copy machine. Aside from saving time, this will allow you the freedom to manipulate pattern sizes in the fabric creating a variety within seconds. Fabrics suitable for appliqué are shown in **photos 1, 2, 3 &4**.

1

2

One of the best additions to a wardrobe is a crinkled vest with appliqué. Cut out the vest one inch larger than the finished size. This allows some freedom for shrinkage and provides the basic size and shape of the pattern. You can easily see the position of the center front, neck edge, and armhole, which prevents you from placing a wonderful design element in a bad spot.

Place a fusible medium on the wrong side of the appliqué fabric (Transfer-Fusing™ or Stitch Witchery® with a pressing sheet). Mark and cut out the appliqué pattern. Position the appliqué on the vest and fuse with the wool setting on a good steam iron. Proper fusing requires steam. Do not over fuse.

Geometric designs enlargement from Chapel House Fabric

continues

**Leaf design enlargement from P&B's
Baltimore Beauties Fabric**

Though this could be a finished project, it is advisable to stitch the edge in some manner. The choices are endless. Use rayon or metallic thread. A satin stitch with a medium to wide zigzag is appropriate. Another idea is to blanket stitch by hand or machine. Change the width and length of the stitch to correspond to the size of the appliqué. Or try stitching to the inside of the appliqué (on page 12) with a straight stitch or narrow zigzag, forcing the outer edge of the appliqué to fray and ravel.

Woven or knitted fabrics are suitable for appliqué. The faux suedes such as Ultra Suede® and Lamous,® make wonderful appliqué. Choose the appliqué fabric for the appearance desired. Color — shiny, dull, napped and textured — play a part in the finished look. A small

5

portion of a color can highlight the finished design. Do not plan to match colors exactly as that can lead to frustration. It is okay to have a slightly off color in the same project. I once used tomato red, burgundy red, and blue red in the same project. There was not a tremendous amount of any one of the colors, just enough to draw the eye to each section. By adding stitches and changing the width and length of the stitch, rather than using a standard satin stitch, you can begin a boundless exploration into the use of appliqué.

6

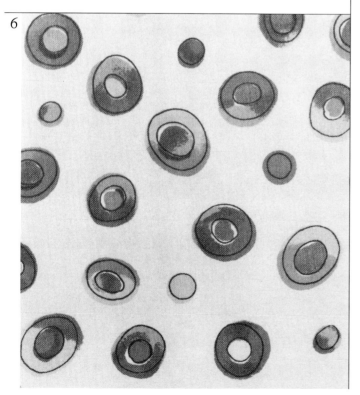

*J*ane Hill of Hillcraft Needle Arts has a spiraling procedure that is not only quick, but simple to do. The finished product appears tedious and involved, yet the technique is basic. Long strips are sewn together, folded and stitched into a tube. She cuts the tube, producing a larger strip piece with a variety of short strips attached in a bias design. This is a variation of the scarf technique used in previous years.

With a variety of colors and a combination of light, medium, and dark fabrics, sew several 45 inch strips (width of fabric) together using ¼ inch seam allowances **(photo 1)**. Mixed widths from 1 to 2 inch cut strips at ¼ inch increments make an effective design. Cut some strips 1 inch when a minimal amount of that color is desired. Cut other strips 1¼, 1½, or 1¾ inches depending upon the design in the fabric or the amount of color desired. With ¼ inch seam allowances throughout, the finished strip is ½ inch narrower than the cut strip. Feel free to use small mismatched strips of color. It is amazing how a small portion of a contrasting color can add spark to a project.

The long strips stitched together should be at least 5 to 6 inches wide for the spiraling to work easily. The wider the main strip the easier it is to continue with the spiraling procedure on the sewing machine. Press the seams towards the darker strip.

Using a see-thru ruler and a rotary cutter, square both ends of the strip. Accuracy is important. Beginning with a right angle makes future steps more precise. A crooked cut edge and seam causes future seams to be slightly off.

With the sewn strips lying flat on a surface, fold one corner over to the side to form a bias angle **(photo 2)**. Place pin in the

1

continues

¼ inch seam at the corner. Pivot the corner to align the longer straight edges. Start sewing these ¼ inch seams together, forming a spiraling effect until reaching the end of the strip (**photo 3**). This step forms a tube with pointed edges extending from both ends (**photo 4**).

When the seam is complete, make a press line along one side of the fold. Cut along this fold to expose a larger piece of parallel strips.

Make a second strip identical to the first and square the ends. To begin the spiraling on the second strip, fold the fabric in the opposite direction.

continues

Continue as before. This second strip will be spiraled at a mirror image or opposite angle to the first.

Cut strips of these diagonal pieces to insert between sections of a garment or place one of each angle beside the other to produce a zigzag design (**photo 5**). Evenly cut strips produce a zigzag design; however, a pattern combining uneven narrow and wide strips produces a hills & valleys appearance.

Sew two pieces together with ¼ inch seam allowances matching the strips. Accuracy is important in this technique. To eliminate the need for perfection, however, you may insert a row of corded piping or beading with ribbon to break

4

the diagonal seams (**page 23**). The options are endless. The patterns can match or they can be entirely different. There are some basic rules to follow, but the focus is to surprise yourself by quickly creating a wonderful, quickly pieced section.

5

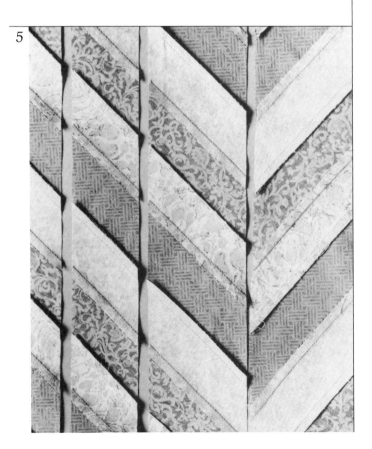

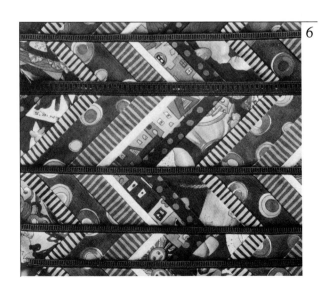

6

LATTICE PIECING

I may never make a quilt, but I adore the combinations of fabrics, colors, and designs used in quilts today. Many of the techniques used in quilting also translate well to sewing garments and accessories. I want to try as many of the piecing patterns as I possibly can, using them on a smaller scale than in quilting.

Many designers make templates or puzzle pieces for their quilt and build them into a wonderful larger piece. Others have quicker ideas. They take fine fabric, cut it up and sew it together. Then they may cut it and sew it back together again. By shuffling the pieces as they are re-stitched, these designers form unique patterns. This type of sewing can be used to create either traditional piecing or contemporary designs. The modern term for this process of cutting–sewing, cutting–sewing is known as quick piecing.

Sewing has monopolized much of my time. Whenever possible I take classes from other teachers as inspiration and to enhance my skills. I always add my taste to their concept. One inspiring teacher is Jude Larzelere. Her techniques are used in my garment for Statements 1992.

Because this piecing shrinks tremendously you should begin with a base fabric at least 1½ times the finished size. The base fabric is crinkled in photograph; however, it could be flat. Cut the base fabric lengthwise every 2 to 4 inches **(step 1)**. Insert cut strips approximately 1 to 2 inches wide using ¼ inch seam allowances. Press the seams towards the darker fabric. Alternately, when the base fabric is crinkled, press towards the inserted piece.

The next cutting is diagonal lines from one direction **(step 2)**. This is not a true bias, but somewhere in the general area. The cutting lines are spaced approximately 3 to 4 inches apart. The insert strips should be slightly narrower than the first insert strips. As the strips are inserted, shift the base piece up or down

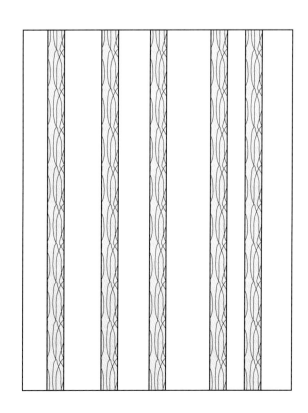

1

continues

so the previous seams do not match. The first narrow strips will be chopped into different shapes and sizes to form new dimensions. Press towards the inserted strip.

Continuing to the third insert strip, cut the base fabric in the opposite direction (**step 3**). This is not a true bias. The cutting lines are spaced about 2½ to 5 inches apart. The inserted strips are narrower than the previous strips. This section could be entredeux beading (Combining the Elements chapter). Again, as the strips are stitched back together, avoid matching the cross sections. The base fabric and added strips will continue to be cut into bits.

The final insert is the smallest. The

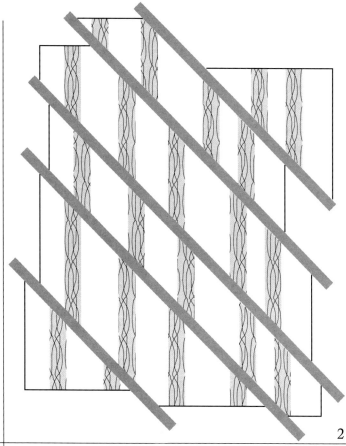

2

3

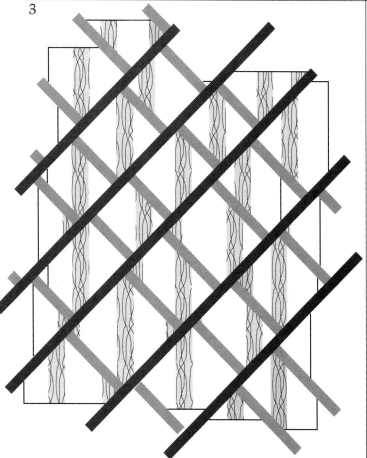

base fabric is cut at several angles, but none of the cuts intersect each other (**step 4**). The narrower the strip, the more difficult it is to achieve evenness. The narrow beading sews in perfectly because the edge stitching foot guides the needle position. Just as before, the sections are not aligned as stitched.

This piecing technique is beautiful with solid color fabric as well as a combination solid and figured fabric. The base could be crinkled, figured fabric with additional solid and/or figured fabrics. Let your imagination run wild. Add a strip of lamé. Use an embroidery insertion. There are no set rules.

These steps with color photography are on pages 24 & 25.

continues on page 31

Technique is basic… spiraling creates
many different patterns

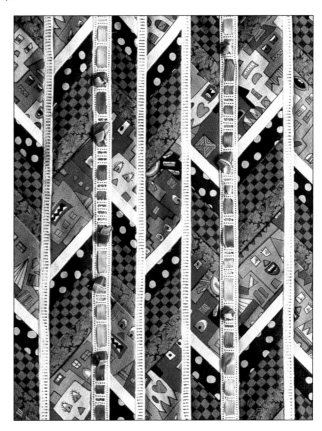

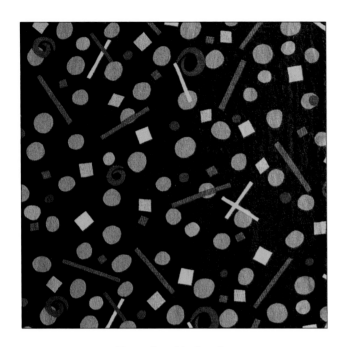

Basic Fabric

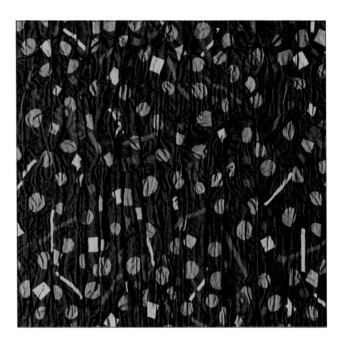

Crinkling

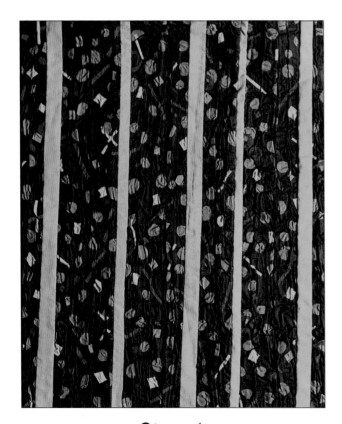

Step 1

Step 2

Step 3

Step 4

Lattice piecing produced with
P&B Fabric combined with
Capitol Imports entredeux
beading and faggoting
buttons by JHB

Using the Folkwear Hungarian Szür Pattern as a base, various embellishment techniques and heirloom methods were used to create "Mixed Media" by Linda McGehee

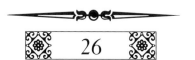

Designed for Statements, an invitational show debuting at 1992 Portland Quilt Market

Lining pieced with leftover fabric

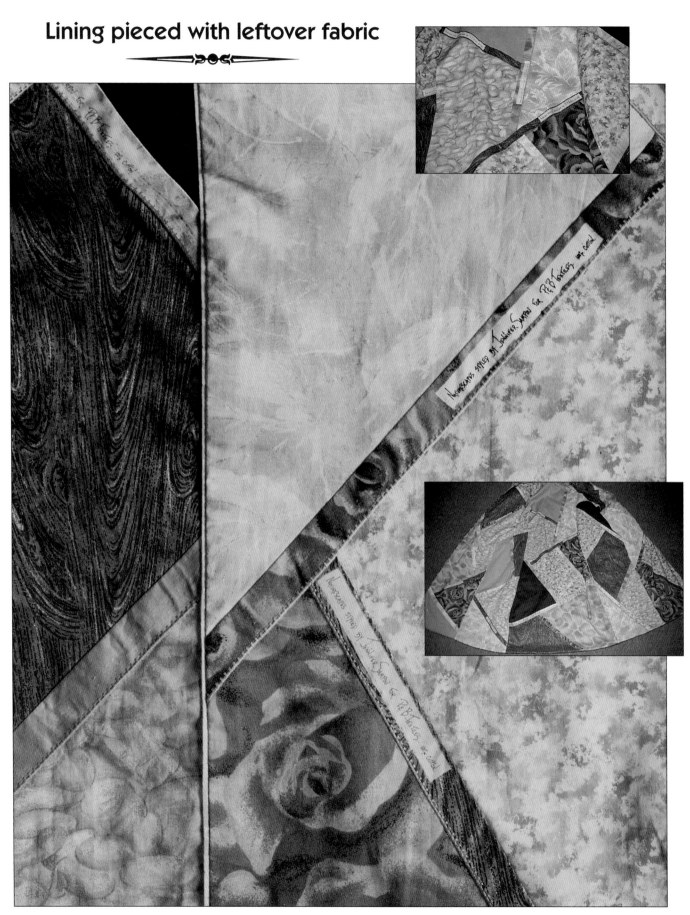

A Ghee's handbag to match,
created from scraps

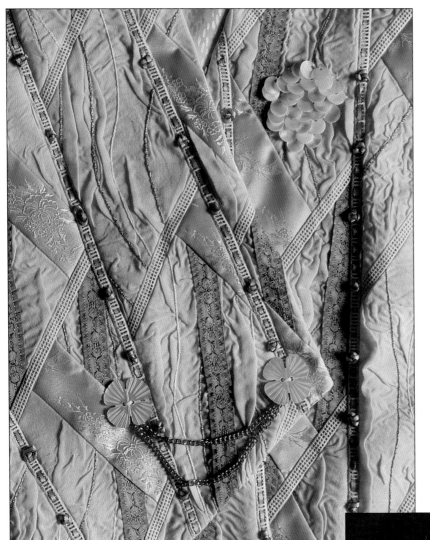

Crinkled handkerchief
linen and wool challis
combined with ribbon,
couching and faggoting
create quite an illusion
All from Capitol Imports

Handbag chain from
Ghee's adds decorative
touch to buttons by JHB

continued from page 22

Extra Tips for Lattice Piecing

❀ Black is an excellent base to use with a variety of high contrast strips.

❀ A tone on tone design does not show the technique as well as accent colors for the different insets. Pastels are as pretty as jewel tones. Vary the colors in the design.

❀ A ½ inch or wider ribbon could be used instead of an inserted strip for step 1. To maintain a straight line machine baste ribbon on base fabric and couch in position using a decorative stitch or combination of stitches on the machine.

❀ When a solid color is used for the base, couch a heavier metallic thread or narrow ribbon before cutting the first step.

❀ Label strips when cutting to maintain proper sequence.

4

5

❀ Place strips at varying distances. They may be parallel or slightly off. Change the angle of cuts for different appearances.

❀ Try to accentuate breaks in color. Do not match strips at seams.

❀ To prevent stretching the fabric on the bias always place the accent color on top.

❀ Press the seams towards the darker strip unless the bulk of crinkling or beading prevents pressing flat.

MINIATURES

*M*iniature quilts
have become popular in the
quilting industry. Another of
my quilting friends, Kathie Johnson has
authored the book, *Smaller and Smaller*, on
the subject of miniatures. Though I may
never make a miniature wall hanging or
quilt for my dolls bed, I enjoy incorporat-
ing the smaller traditional quilt blocks
into my wearable art garments.

To make the blocks easier and more
accurate, Kathie uses a paper backing to
form the designs. The paper works best
because the designs are so tiny that it is
difficult to handle the small pieces of
fabric. The paper acts as a base to prevent

Wrong Side of Pattern

1

2

shifting. There is no reason to worry with
grainline since the pieces are so tiny.

One of the traditional designs, flying
geese, works well as a vertical line in a
garment. It also works as a connector for
horizontal lines. Because it is the quickest
design to do, it is the one chosen to use in
these garments.

Several sizes of the flying geese are
included **(page 35)**. Feel free to use a copy
machine to reproduce the designs rather
than drawing them for **your own per-
sonal projects**. Keep in mind that copy
machines by law must distort the image
they produce. Double check the repro-
duction for accuracy.

Be sure to use the size with a proportion suitable for the design in the garment. Consider enlarging or reducing this design on a copy machine. You may want to use 2 or 3 rows of smaller geese, placing one row in one direction and another row in the other direction. Feel free to experiment with the geese. They can fly north, east, south or west!

Because the design is so small, tiny bits of highly contrasted fabric work beautifully. Shades that are similar tend to blend rather than show workmanship. Larger prints lose their pattern. Smaller ones add more detail. Study fabrics before cutting them. Be certain the color differs between #1, and #2 and #3 on the

3

4

pattern. Sometimes the larger prints will offer a variety of color without requiring the use of different fabrics. Lightweight fabrics adapt to miniatures because of the sizes of the finished pieces. Once you start working with miniatures, your scrap box will contain the smallest fabric pieces.

To begin the geese pattern, copy the design on paper. Be sure to include a ¼ inch seam allowance around the marked design. Fabric is placed on the unprinted side of the paper pattern. Stitching is done on the printed side of the pattern. Stitching should be tiny (1½) for durability. It also perforates the paper for easy removal. The stitching should extend 3 to 4 stitches beyond the stitching line. Because the

continues

pattern included is short, tape several strips together matching the design lines when a longer strip is desired.

The first fabric is placed on the unprinted side of the pattern right side out, covering the piece marked #1 (**photo 1**). Use the water soluble glue stick to hold the fabric in position and prevent slipping. Using a contrasting or background fabric with right sides together cover piece adjacent to #2. Turn unit over and stitch along the printed line between piece #1 and #2, remembering to extend the stitching beyond the printed line (**photo 2**). Trim excess fabric in seam allowance to ⅛ inch and flip remaining fabric to cover #2 piece (**photo 3**). Finger press into place.

Using the same fabric as #2, position the right side of the fabric to cover piece beside #3 (**photo 4**). Follow the stitch, trim, flip and press procedure. The sec-

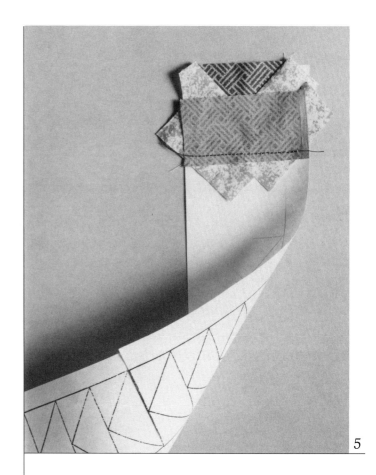

5

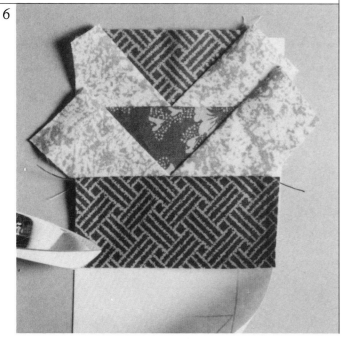

6

ond #1 piece is placed right sides together covering the previous goose pattern, allowing a minimal of fabric in the seam allowance (**step 5**). Stitch along the longer stitch line between the 2 patterns. Again follow the trim, flip and press procedure to continue the flying geese pattern (**step 6**).

After the strip is completed, trim along the dashed lines of the paper pattern. This is a ¼ inch seam allowance. To prevent stretching out of shape do not remove any paper until the strip is attached to another fabric piece.

Many traditional miniature quilt patterns can be incorporated into garments

*T*he possibilities for embellishment are endless, but occasionally a basic garment is desired—garment that can be worn as a basic, yet can be transformed into a variety of looks, much like changing jewelry. An inset permits a variety of changes, from a collection of buttons, a miniature quilt block, machine or hand embroidery, charted needlework, a collection of laces or embroideries, cross stitch, needlepoint or other hand work would permit diversity in one garment.

Vests are always in fashion. They complete an ensemble and are considered an accessory. What about a vest with an interchangeable inset? A vest with a basic fabric and an inset would be simple to make. Yet when time allowed, other embellishments could be incorporated into the inset.

The best place to position the inset is the left shoulder in the area of a handkerchief pocket. The top of the interchangeable opening should be approximately 4½ to 5 inches from the shoulder seam for a woman. The position may change with a child's or man's garment; however, the lower edge of the opening should be higher than the lowest edge of the armscye. This technique may be used on the back of a jacket, the side of a hand-bag or wherever you wish.

Base the size and shape you use on the amount of fabric in the shoulder area. Several oval options are shown **(pattern 1 & 2)** but perhaps a circle would show the design better. The shape may be altered and the size may be enlarged or reduced. Determine how much working area there is taking seam allowances into consideration. There must be at least 1½ inches on all sides of the opening for the interchangeable idea to work properly.

Select a fabric to use as a mock cording. The finished opening looks as though much time

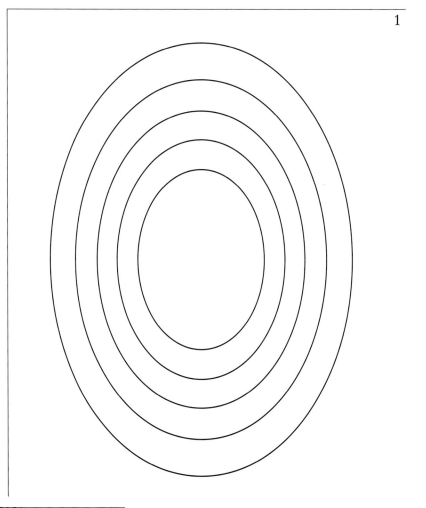

1

was spent constructing corded piping, but the basic concept is simply a facing. To make the mock cording, cut an 8 inch square of the facing fabric. Or as patterns vary, cut a rectangle 1 inch wider than the armhole to neck edge and as deep as the opening, plus 3 inches. Contrasting fabric may be used to show definition. Fabric matching the basic fabric may be used when the mock cording is subtle. Or the wrong side of the fabric may be used when a slight change is desired. This idea works beautifully with denim, which is great on both sides. When a contrasting fabric is difficult to find, perhaps the wrong side of the fabric would be more suitable for the mock corded piping!

Position the right side of the cording fabric on the right side of the fashion fabric. Use a washable marker or pencil of some type to mark the exact size of the opening on the wrong side of the facing fabric.

2

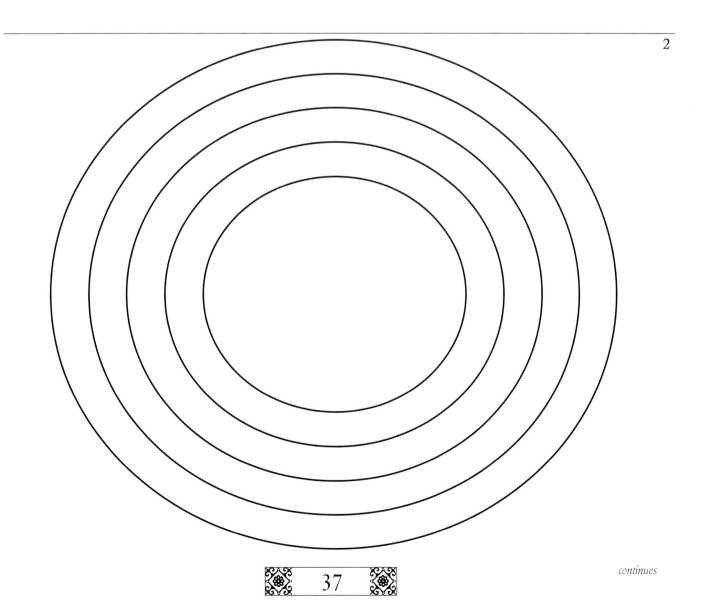

continues

Mark the exact size of the opening on the mock cording piece. Use a short stitch length (1½ to 2) to stitch around the oval. Overlap ending with beginning stitches to secure and avoid bulk (photo 3). Trim to ¹⁄₁₆ inch but no wider than ⅛ inch (photo 4).

Turn cording fabric through hole to allow just an edge (no more than ⅛ inch) of cording fabric to show (**photo 5**). Stitch in the ditch with the edge stitching foot to hold cording in place (**photo 6**). The edge stitching foot works better than the open toe foot because the tiny edging on the foot aligns perfectly with the

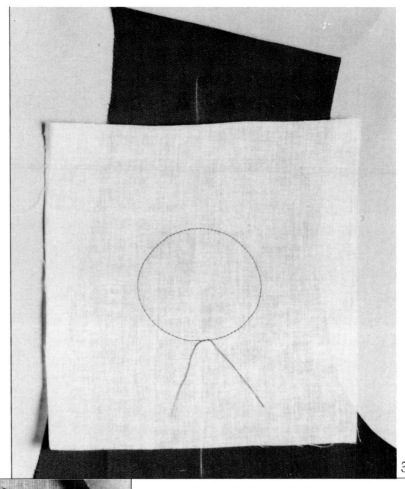

3

4

corded area. The narrow trimmed seam allowance fills the cording area, making the ridge look as though there is a cord in the area.

Steam press the opening to maintain shape. On the wrong side of the corded hole, measure the size of the cording facing the fabric. Cut a lining fabric that is ½ inch shorter than the height of the facing (**photo 7**). The lining extends to within ¼ inch above and ¼ inch below, facing equally over the opening. Choose a fusible interfacing that is light and soft. The interfacing should not be stiff or bulky. French fuse™ is a recommended weight. Cut fusible interfacing at least 1 inch larger than the facing section. Place fusible interfacing over complete mock cording section and lining to hold the interchangeable pocket in place (**photo 8**). Use the wool setting with heavy steam to hold the interfacing in place with the other sections. Trim excess mock cording fabric, inset fabric and interfacing along the vest cutting lines (**photo 9**).

In the case of a narrow section on a garment, extend the lining to the neck and armhole edge.

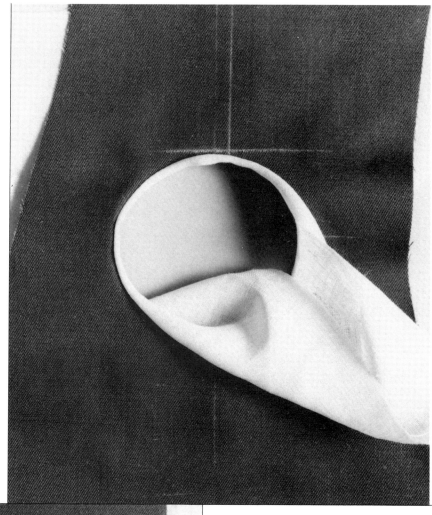

5

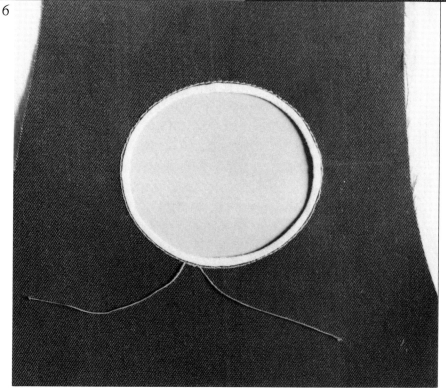

6

Determine the pocket size formed by these steps. This is the size for the base fabric to be used for future insets. Mark the opening size on the base fabric and embellish galore—buttons, beads, sequins, rhinestones, traditional or contemporary piecing, appliqué, heirloom sewing, pin tucking, couching, crinkling, charted needlework, embroidery, cross-stitch, needlepoint—and away we go.

continues

7

8

9

An inset permits a variety of changes–from a collection of buttons, a miniature quilt block, machine or hand embroidery, charted needlework, a collection of laces or embroideries, cross stitch, needle point or other hand work–that permit diversity in one garment

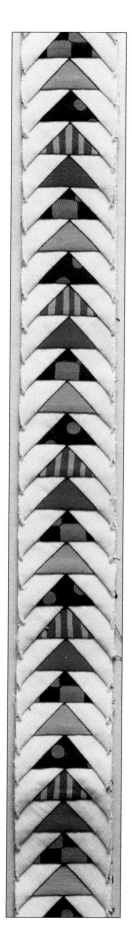

Two satin ribbons layered together are
woven randomly through the beading
with an occasional knot or flower

Though it looks like tedious corded piping, the cameo is simply a facing

Miniatures add a touch of "traditional" to wearable arts

P&B Fabrics and Wamsutta Fabrics offer many groupings suitable for creating texture combined with miniatures, spiraling ,couching, pintucks and the cameo

Experiments can be inserted and interchanged in the cameo shuffle

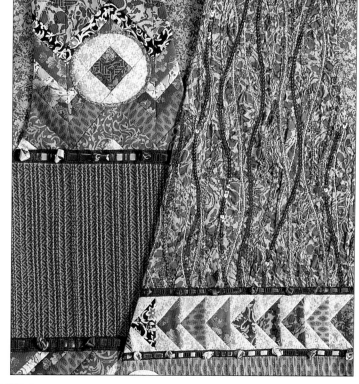

Ghee's handbags with additional insets created from leftovers

*F*requently an extra touch of dimension is desired. A rhinestone, button or sequin will not do. But something is necessary to fill a void in a space. Fuzzies and tassels qualify for this position. They are simple to create and the color limitations come from the variety of threads available. Threads that ravel, such as the heavier metallic and rayon threads, work beautifully for either technique. A combination of threads in a variety of colors produces the best design, depending on the project.

To make a fuzzy, twist 10 to 20 threads together to form a cord (**step 1**). It is easiest to begin with several long pieces of thread, fold them in half and then in half again.

To prevent pulling the finished fuzzy apart, use the open-toe foot with a serpentine stitch, a short length and width as wide as the cord, to stitch the distance eventually intended for the satin stitch (**step 2**). With the presser foot down, set the machine for a perfect satin stitch the width

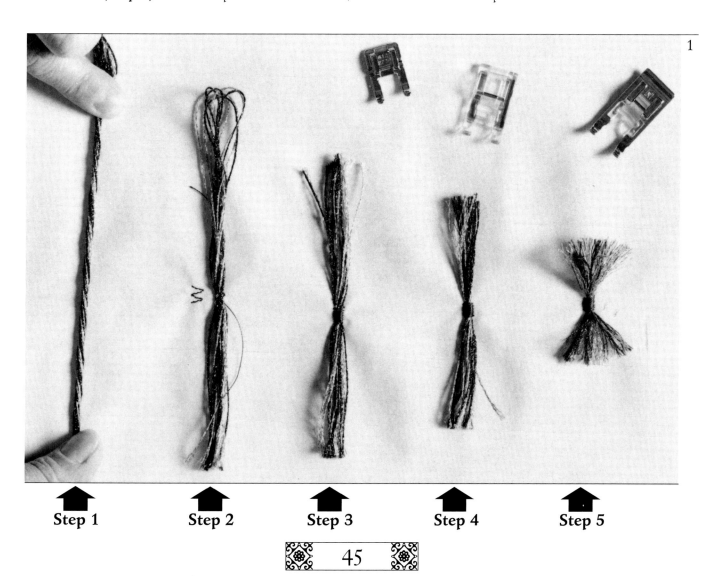

1

Step 1   Step 2   Step 3   Step 4   Step 5

of the cord. While in reverse, stitch over the serpentine stitch to the beginning of the stitching (**step 3**). Set the width just a little wider and stitch forward over all previous stitches to achieve a smooth finish (**step 4**). Because of the bulk of threads consider helping the machine during the final stitching.

Once the stitching is complete, trim the fuzzies to the desired length (**step 5**). Using your hands, brush over the threads causing them to ravel and fuzz. The shorter threads look different from longer threads. The amount of original threads produce different effects. Again, experiment, set a rhythm, and begin production of fuzzies.

Tassels are somewhat easier, perhaps because one step is omitted. Begin with twisted threads, as with the fuzzies (**step A**). Zigzag over these threads about ¼ inch (**step B**). Sink the needle into the fabric, lift the presser foot, pull the upper twisted threads around to position them on top of the others, and satin stitch over the previous stitching (**step C**). Widen the stitch when necessary. Trim to desired length (**step D**). Let the threads hang naturally or use your hands to mingle and separate them. Tassels have never been easier.

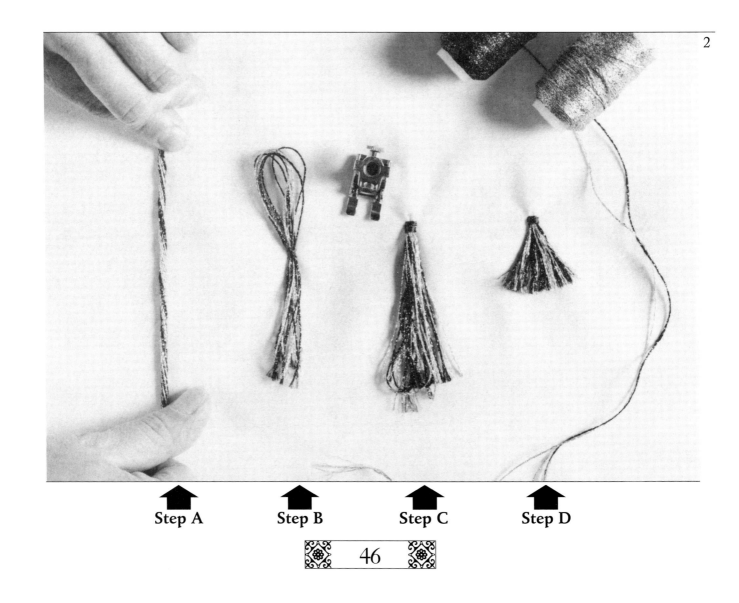

Step A   Step B   Step C   Step D

COMBINING THE ELEMENTS

O ne of the pleasures of sewing today is the assortment of equipment, tools, and decorative notions available to make any task easier and more fun to complete. Though the time element is a factor, there are options to this dilemma. Experiment with the sewing machine on small projects. Or, take a few minutes to try a new technique on less fabric. These smaller pieces can be combined to form a larger section on a garment. When combining elements to form one project, consider not only the basic corded piping from **Texture With Textiles**, but some of the other ideas in this chapter.

Beading

An option in joining sections of a garment, yet maintaining definition between the different types of work, is to use entredeux beading or faggoting in the seams between the sections. This type of beading is basically a batiste with embroidery stitching to form slits through which ribbon can be laced.

Normally the extra batiste on the edges of the beading is trimmed away. In some instances, that is the proper way to sew it. However, to combine sections of a garment that are bulky and cannot be rolled, as in heirloom sewing (**Texture With Textiles**), this is the easiest and quickest method. This technique works best with straight seams. Because the width of the beading, it is difficult to curve the seams.

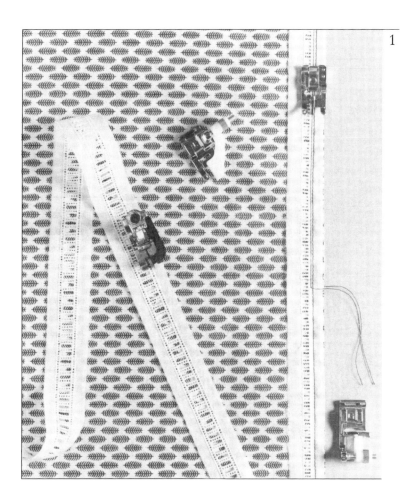
1

2

continues

47

3

With the beading on top, right sides together, match the cut edge of the batiste with the cut edge of the garment. Align the bar of the edge stitching foot to the right ridge of the beading (photo 1). This will act as a guide, making the stitching position accurate. Move the needle position to the right and stitch approximately $\frac{1}{16}$ of an inch from the ridge. The small distance between the last ridge of the beading and the stitching allows the beading to turn. Known as the turn of the fabric, this technique helps maintain a flat seam. All of the beading will be exposed and little bulk will remain in the seam allowance.

The original design for beading was to guide ribbon evenly through the holes, weaving in a patterned manner. There is no rule that states that the weaving pattern must be symmetrical. Or if there is a rule, now is the time to break it! Guide the ribbon with a tapestry needle under some of the slits and over others. Do not establish a balanced design. Go over one, under three, over two, under five or whatever strikes your fancy (photo 2). Remember, it's okay to break the rules. Every once in awhile, tie a knot or make a bow (photo 3). Allow the design and color of the ribbon to add dimension. Use two layers of ribbon through the same slits. When the knot is tied the colors will flip, making a two-toned section. Make a mistake once in awhile. The mistake may lead to a better arrangement than the original plan!

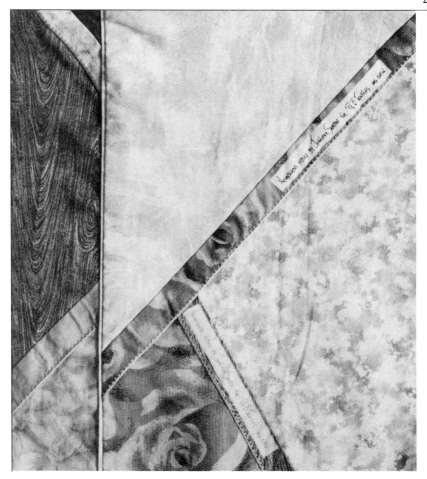

4

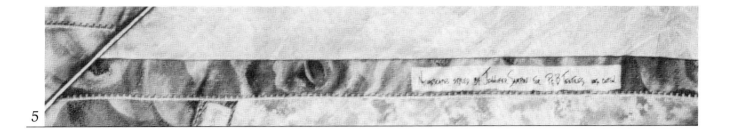

Inserting a Strip

Occasionally a problem arises because there is a minimum of fabric for a garment and a lining is necessary. Though a lining wears better when it is slippery, other fabrics may be used. For instance, this lining is the same as the outer fabric only in the flat position. It is a cotton that does not slide well against other cottons, but it is usable as a lining. There is no embellishment to add bulk to the inside of the garment. Though the garment may not slide onto the body, the inside is as intriguing as the outside.

Because there was not enough fabric, the lining was pieced with the leftover fabrics. A puzzle was drawn on the lining. To join pieces, a strip of fabric along the selvage (including the designer's name) was incorporated between the sections **(photo 4)**. Sometimes there is space to include a ¼ inch seam allowance. Other times the seams must be overlapped and stitched with a decorative stitch. In this instance, the stretch stitch with maximum width combined with a satin stitch was used on the selvage edge and ¼ inch seam allowance on the cut side. Contrasting thread in the bobbin with the tensions tightened made a special design **(photo 5)**.

6

Gathered Corded Piping

Corded piping adds dimension and definition to seams and edges. It separates one section of design work from another, giving the design its own framework.

Continuous bias and basic corded piping were illustrated in **Texture With Textiles**. To make a gathered corded piping, position the cording in the center of the bias strip. Though a bias strip is desired for stripes and plaids, the crosswise

continues

grain can be used when fabric is minimal. Because many gathers are included with the piping, the cording easily rounds curves and corners.

Fold the strip in half over the cording. Stitch with the cording or piping foot using the far right needle position on the machine (photo 6). This stitching will appear approximately ⅛ to ¹⁄₁₆ of an inch from the cord, allowing the cord to slip freely through the bias.

Before gathering the piping with the cording, mark the garment sections in quarters or eighths. Decide how much fullness you want in the cording—usually 1½ times to 2 times is enough. Then mark the piping fabric accordingly (photo 7). Pull the cording to form gathers on the

7

8

piping, matching the corresponding marks on the garment. Evenly distribute the gathers between marks. Stitch the gathered corded piping to the garment with the needle position closer to the corded piping (photo 8). Continue to add the next garment section to the corded piping.

This type of corded piping is particularly nice around pin tucks, heirloom sewing and any area that is not crinkled. The gathered corded piping sometimes loses its identity when placed next to wrinkled fabric, though you may consider it an option.

Remember, there are no set rules

*T*here are an assortment of feet available for the sewing machine to make the task easier, more accurate, and less stressful on the eyes. Ask your dealer for the feet that correspond to the techniques that you use. Your sewing will become precise and more fun. The following list includes feet that I use constantly with my sewing.

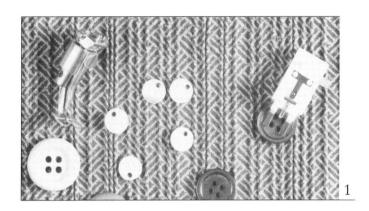

1

Braiding Foot: A hole at the front of the foot is large enough to guide small braid, heavier twisted threads, ribbon, yarn or cords, making couching a simple embellishment. Under the foot is a small groove that permits the bulk of the threads to pass without a buildup of stitches. A simple zigzag as well as decorative stitches may be applied. Several sizes may be available for the same machine.

Button Sew on Foot: This foot is used to sew on buttons with a zigzag machine making button sewing a breeze rather than a chore **(photo 1)**. Many feet have adjustable bars to sew shanks with ease.

Cording Foot with 3, 5, or 7 Grooves: The different cording feet are used primarily to embroider several heavier threads at once, resulting in a multicolored design much like a narrow ribbon. The different holes or grooves align the threads perfectly. Practical or decorative stitches produce special effects.

2

Creative Feet: Designed by a sewing expert for embellishment applications, these feet make sewing a breeze. The Satinedge™ Foot is for appliqué, top stitching, and edge stitching. Sew ¼ inch sequins, ribbons, ric-rac, and elastic with the Sequins 'N Ribbons™ Foot. And use the Pearls 'N Piping™ Foot for beads, pearls, corded piping and decorative cords. Feet are available to fit most machines.

Edge Stitch or Joining Foot: Normally used to guide the work for accurate edge stitching or top stitching along the seams of a garment, some feet have an adjustable guide to accommodate various widths while others require changing the needle position. The foot can also be used to combine laces and embroidery trims, or appliqué with ribbons or braids.

Little Foot: Designed by a quilter for piecing, this foot is ¼ inch from center needle position to right edge which creates an accurate ¼ inch seam allowance. Notches allow a perfect position for starting, stopping and pivoting. The left side of the foot is ⅛ inch from center, allowing better control for easing curved piecing, miniatures and stuffed animals or dolls. This foot attaches to most machines.

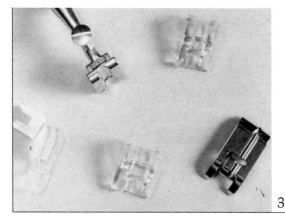

3

Open Toe Embroidery Foot: Intended for appliqué and embroidery, this foot has a small flat groove underneath allowing the bulk of threads to pass to the back of the foot without a buildup of stitches **(photo 2)**. The open toe permits excellent visibility of all curves and corners for accurate stitching. A double use for the foot is couching ¼ inch ribbon and sequins, which fit perfectly between the toes of the foot.

Pin Tucking Feet: Designed with a series of 3 to 9 grooves underneath, these feet are used with a double needle to produce perfect uniform tucks. Consecutive parallel rows are stitched by placing the first tuck under one of the grooves in the foot. Use different grooves in the foot or decorative stitches for special effects. Double check the stitch width to be certain the needle clears the presser foot. Different size needles combined with different grooved feet make tucks in a variety of sizes.

Piping Foot: Designed to sew on corded piping, this foot contains a large hollowed groove on the bottom to facilitate heavier cords, beads and pearls, allowing them to lie flat and glide easily along the bottom of the foot **(photo 3)**. Adjust the needle position to the size cord used.

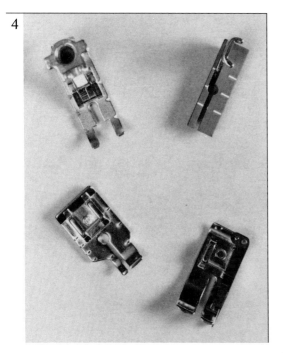

4

Teflon Foot: Similar in appearance to the basic foot from the upper side, this foot has a coating of Teflon on the bottom to allow non-slippery fabrics like suede and plastic to glide under the foot rather than sticking to it.

Transparent Embroidery Foot: This foot looks very much like the open toe foot with the same features, except there is a transparent section before the needle hole. These two feet may be interchanged. Consider it a matter of preference.

¼ Inch Foot: Designed for accuracy with patchwork, this foot has markings for perfect ¼ inch and ⅛ inch seam allowances **(photo 4)**. Other markings on the foot permit precision corners as well as beginning and ending at the exact ¼ inch point.